T0247192

NICCI WILLIS, MBA

LAS VEGAS
REAL ESTATE
AGENT

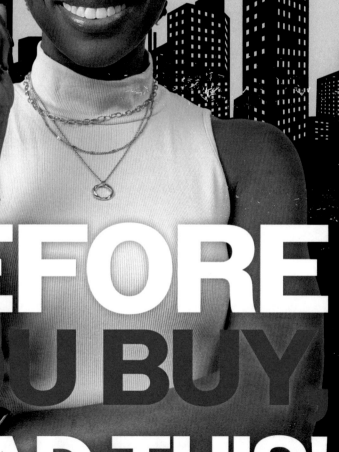

BEFORE
YOU BUY
READ THIS!

HOME OWNERSHIP MADE EASY

This book is intended for edutainment purposes only. While it provides valuable insights and guidance on homeownership, it should not be considered individual professional advice. Readers are encouraged to consult with their realtor for specific advice tailored to their individual circumstances. By using this book, you remain a customer, not a client.

Before You Buy, Read This!
Home Ownership Made Easy
Nicci Willis, MBA

ISBN (Print Edition): 979-8-35096-594-0
ISBN (eBook Edition): 979-8-35096-595-7

**This book is dedicated to all of
my past clients... thank you!**

NOT YOUR TYPICAL HOME BUYING BOOK

Hey there! Welcome to the wild ride of homeownership! Whether you're flipping through these pages with excitement bubbling over or still pondering if now's the time to dive in, you're in good hands. This book is like your trusty sidekick as you dive into one of life's biggest adventures: owning your own slice of heaven.

Getting a home isn't just about snagging some property; it's about investing in your future, your aspirations, and that warm fuzzy feeling of having your own space. It's about crafting a place that screams "you" and tells the story of where you've been and where you're going. And yeah, I get it, it can feel a bit overwhelming at first. But trust me, you've got this. Armed with the right info, a bit of guidance, and a sprinkle of confidence, you'll breeze through each step like a boss!

Whether you're a young professional itching to settle down, a growing family in need of more elbow room, or just someone craving the comfort of calling someplace home sweet home, this book's tailor-made for you. From decoding mortgage mumbo jumbo to scoping out neighborhoods, from haggling over offers to feeling like a boss doing it, I've got your back.

Think of this book not just as a guide, but as a buddy along for the ride to homeownership. We'll toast to your victories, calm those nerves, and arm you with all the knowledge and tools you need to make savvy choices.

So, grab your favorite drink, snuggle up in your favorite nook, and let's dive into this adventure together. Your ideal home is out there, and we're here to make sure you find it. Cheers to new beginnings and the sweet joy of calling a place your own. Welcome home! 🏠

WHO AM I?

I've been in real estate for over 13 years. I started off as a part time transaction coordinator for my husband who is also a realtor (26+ years). I am a homeowner. But I wasn't in previous years. In fact, the first home I owned, I lost during the '09 housing market crash. All I can remember was that buying my first house was a blur. I had help but I was still clueless as to what I was doing. And I was just as clueless as to how I was feeling about being clueless. I promised myself then that if I had the chance to do it over, I would make sure I documented the process to ensure I really understood it. Now that I am in real estate full time, I can not only share the process, but I can also talk about all the "other stuff" nobody talks about that works against you reaching your goal of becoming a homeowner- life setbacks, internal struggles, and a system that was built for only a few to succeed. I have found over the years, addressing both the home buying process along with the "other stuff" helps a potential buyer anticipate what's coming and feel empowered to keep moving forward.

Another thing…I teach on the side! I've been a college professor, a children's Sunday school teacher, and I currently serve as the National Facilitator Trainer for an organization called Mortar which serves and equips entrepreneurs in under-served communities. Basically, I'm really good at taking some of the most complex ideas and making them not only understandable but fun in the process.

I have a background in events. I created and operated my own on-site event childcare company for 10 years. My company would bring highly skilled, trained staff to the location of any event and entertain guests' children, while guests enjoyed themselves stress-free. This wasn't just your average babysitting. We would create entire themed events that children would enjoy. Not only that, we had exactly 2 minutes for a parent to come up to our check-in table and determine whether they were going to trust *perfect strangers* with their children while they attended sales meetings, participated in weddings or partied all night long. How were parents able to trust us with their children and give us glowing reviews even though they had just dropped one of the most, if not, the most important people in the world off to us? It's because the experience began long before they ever met us. We knew how they would feel at each stage:

1. Finding out they could bring their children (elation)

2. Finding out strangers would be babysitting them (skepticism), to doing a deep-dive into our company (discovery), to registering their child (optimistic but still skeptical), to having questions about the quality of service (worry), to finally walking their child up to the check-in booth where they see two smiling faces greeting them by name and mentioning something special the parent wrote in their child's registration profile (reserved optimism).

3. Realizing this event childcare company has far exceeded their initial expectations as they walk into a brightly decorated room with music playing and some very familiar toys and games around. They notice a full evening of activities has been planned along with a meal specified to their child's dietary needs. And as they give their child a hug to see them later, they smile to themselves and feel relief, joy, and excitement. They can now enjoy the full experience at their own event.

Why is this so important? I have developed a keen eye for how people process experiences. *The home buying process is an experience.*

THE HOME-
BUYING PROCESS
IS AN
EXPERIENCE.

According to Clever.com[1], 93% of recent buyers have regrets about their home buying experience — a 29% increase from the 72% who said the same in 2022.

That is a lot of unhappy homeowners! So, friend, if I can anticipate your needs during your home buying experience and give you tips and tricks on how to navigate your journey, would this book be valuable to you? If so, good! This book is for you!

---

1   https://listwithclever.com/research/homebuyer-report-2023

WHY AM I WRITING THIS BOOK?

I'm writing this book because I am passionate about helping people own their homes rather than rent. There's a saying that when you rent, you're paying a mortgage-it's just someone else's mortgage. I'm also tired of watching news and people in the media constantly debate and give these wild statements about the housing market. Most of the statements are half-truths skewed to fit whatever overall feeling they want to project to their audience. It's information overload and the only thing it's doing is keeping more potential homebuyers on the sidelines. Question: have you ever wondered why the people (who already HAVE) are telling those who don't have NOT to get what they ALREADY HAVE?!? Sir! You already own a home! In fact, you own several! But you're telling everyone that it's not a good time to buy? The audacity!

The other reason why I am writing this book is for the number 28. I'm going to give you a couple of stats that made me just plain mad. So here we go:

1. The Black homeownership rate in Las Vegas is 28% which means for every Ten Black Las Vegans, less than three own a home. LESS. THAN. THREE! 1.. 2.. THREE! Now, I hope that got you as fired up as it got me.

2. The Black homeownership rate in the United States, although higher, is only 42%. The Hispanic homeownership rate is only 49% and the Asian homeownership rate is 63%. Compare that to non-Hispanic White Americans at 73%, according to Today's Homeowner which analyzed U.S. Census data.

There's one more reason why I'm writing this book. Generational wealth. Generational wealth refers to assets passed from one generation of the family to the next. In some cases, assets are transferred after death in the form of an inheritance. In others, they are passed to the next generation while the giver is still alive. [2]

Real estate is still one of the best ways to begin your generational wealth journey. Home equity is real. Remember the rent you are paying? You're also paying down someone else's mortgage, thus increasing the equity in their home that they can then use to borrow against for other things like school or a downpayment on another house. Real estate is not a "get-rich-quick" scheme. There are upturns and downturns in the market. But real estate over time has consistently appreciated in value across the county year over year. And, for many, it is the gateway into generational wealth and the ability to leave a legacy for their families.

Home ownership is not for everyone. But let's talk about who it IS for. For those who want to be homeowners, this book is for you. If you are tired of renting and paying someone else's mortgage, this book is for you. If you are tired of living under the thumb of your landlord and want cabinets you can change, carpet you can pull up, or walls you can paint any color other than eggshell white, this book is for you. If you want to begin your generational wealth journey through your home purchase, this book is for you. If you've always wanted to buy a home but just didn't know where or how to begin… or what to expect, this book is for you.

---

2   What is Generational Wealth? Investopedia

AM I READY TO BE A

Homeowner?

☐ I'm tired of paying someone else's mortgage.

☐ I am tired of renting.

☐ I'm tired of dealing with a landlord.

☐ I want to change my cabinets.

☐ I want to change my carpet.

☐ I want to change the color of my walls.

☐ I'm ready to begin my generational wealth journey.

☐ I've always wanted to buy a home but didn't know how.

BEFORE YOU BUY... READ THIS!

If you've checked off any of these, then this book is for you! Let's get started!

MINDSET

MINDSET

You were expecting me to jump right into the home buying process, weren't you? I told you this book was going to be different. My goal is to get you *to* homeownership. In order to do that, it has to be different. First, we're going to address your mindset. Trust me, it'll be fun at best and eye-opening at worst. But you're reading and I got you now... so just trust me!

One thing to consider when thinking about mindset is that our minds are often cluttered with a lot of different things including the thoughts and opinions of others. No shame. Happens to the best of us. But let's first start by addressing some things others (or even yourself) have said about the home buying process. I'm going to share some things I've heard, but let's first start with you. Take a moment to pause here and think about what others have said about buying a house or thoughts you may have had about the process. Got a pen? Jot these down somewhere.

Okay, I'll tell you some of the things I've heard. Now, keep in mind, this is regardless of whether I have been in a formal consultation with clients, chatting it up with friends or just ear hustling on the streets. You do it too. Don't judge me. But the majority of what I hear is:

"My process was so stressful!"

"I felt so alone in the process!"

"I had no idea what was going on!"

"My realtor never called me! They just put me on some search!"

"I was so confused the whole time!"

"My cousin just bought a house and hated it! That's why I'm not doing it!"

"The loan officer kept bothering me and wanted so much from me!"

"My boss is buying a house right now and she's having a terrible time."

"I didn't know how much it was going to cost me. The number kept changing!"

Do any of these sound familiar? Go ahead and add your list to mine. Now, I want you to mentally press the "reset button" and create a clean slate for this experience. Remember, your experience is just that- yours. You make what you want of it. Now we need to determine if you want to buy a home or if you're ready to buy a home.

From "I want to buy" to "I'm ready to buy"

How many times have we said that we've "wanted" to do something? Maybe you've said something like "I want to go back to school" or "I want to go after that promotion" or "I want to visit another country". Maybe there's something you've always wanted to do that doesn't cost much, take up too much time or requires a big-life change; like learning a new language, learning to ride a bike, or committing to reading one book a month. How many times have we left that "something" standing there waiting to get done? I know. I know. Feel the feels, my friend. I've done it too. Too many times to even count. Now let me ask you (rhetorical of course) how many times have you told yourself or someone else "I want to buy a house in the next [insert number of months here]" and you didn't do it? Don't say it! It's rhetorical!! It's okay, your secret is safe with me.

I get it. There's a lot at stake here. Buying a house is one of, if not the biggest, purchases you'll ever make in your life. There are tons of moving parts. The interest rate won't sit still. Don't even get me started on the news and media. Oh and did I mention life is still "life-ing" out here with bills to pay, family, work, and all the things? WAIT! Before you shut this book and walk away, what if I showed you a better way to navigate that and the home buying process? Would you keep reading? Yes? Then let's go!

You Don't Really "Want" to

Quite frankly I think we use the word "want" too loosely. The dictionary definition "want" means to "have a desire to possess or do something; to wish for". Another informal definition is an "ought, should or need to do something". Now, let's look at the word "ready". The definition of that word literally means "in a suitable state for an activity, action, or situation; fully prepared". Now let's look at these two words in terms of buying a home. A desire or a wish will only take you so far. We just talked about life and all the things that are still going on while you're going to make one of the largest purchases of your life. You wish? *WISH*?!? You desire? *DESIRE*?!? What do you think is going to happen with that wish? It will be sitting there for years to come. Now, let's look at "ready". That definition said "fully prepared"... in a "suitable state for ACTION". *Now* we're talking! Which word sounds like it's set to face whatever comes its way? Which word sounds like it has done the work and is equipped with what is needed? Which word sounds like a decision has been made and it's primed to take action? Do you *want* to buy a house or are you *READY* to buy a house? GREAT! Then let's get you there!

The 3 W's of Home buying

There's one more exercise I want to take you through before we get into some real keys to buying a house. After countless discovery calls and meetings with potential clients, I came to learn that there were only three things a buyer really needs to buy a house. In fact, when I teach my home ownership seminar **H.O.M.E. with Nicci**, this is the first exercise I do in my seminar. I ask the question "What are the three things a buyer needs to buy a house?" Most people say it's money or financing, a good credit score, or something like location. Actually, it's none of these things. And because you're reading this book (and you're my favorite), I'm going to give you the answers.

A buyer needs their Why, Wisdom, and their Will.

Don't look so underwhelmed! Let me explain. First, you need to understand, these three things are interdependent. You can't have one without the others. And the lack of one thing will forfeit your goal in some way. Let's break each one down and look at what happens if you don't have it.

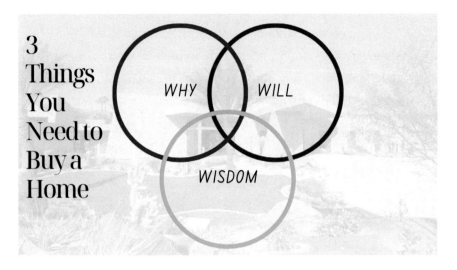

3
Things
You
Need to
Buy a
Home

WHY   WILL

WISDOM

WHY

Everyone usually has their WHY. Your WHY is your reasoning or purpose for doing what you are doing. I like to even call it your "vision" (but Vision starts with a "V" and it messed with my "W" theme... so go with me here). Your WHY guides you during your home buying process. It helps you determine if you need that 5-bedroom with a pool overlooking the Vegas Strip or if a 3-bed-room, in a cul-de-sac with a community pool will be more ideal.

Now, what happens if you don't have your "WHY" (or your vision). If you don't have your WHY you'd end up just buying anything. Your buying process would have no reasoning behind it and no purpose. You'd most likely end up with something you're unhappy with or worse yet, something someone else has convinced you to buy. Cue buyer's remorse. I'm sure you've seen it before. The friend or family member who lost track of their WHY and bought a house with "potential" even though it truly didn't meet the needs that they were originally seeking. Now you're at the Thanksgiving table listening to them complain six months into the purchase about all the things they hate about their house. And all you want them to do is pass the gravy! Your WHY drives what you will and won't say yes or no to. And don't get me wrong. I totally understand compromises and buying for the life you are living in that moment (Because again… life is constantly life-ing). But if you are confident in your WHY you will be pleased with the timing and decision of your purchase.

WISDOM

You need WISDOM. This one is easy. You've got me! Well, not just me. I'm not that vain (maybe just a little). But you do need an excellent real estate team that will guide you in the process. The good thing about this process is that you don't have to know everything about buying a home. You just need to be connected with those who do. And it's not just a realtor either. You need an excellent loan officer that is solution-oriented when it comes to mortgages. Realtors and loan officers work hand-in-hand. I have a whole section on this later where I'll break down your entire real estate team and how to have not just a good team but a *great* team.

Now, what happens if you don't have Wisdom? I can guarantee you will feel alone and confused in your home buying process. Ultimately this will lead to frustration. Did I mention that this is one of the biggest purchases of your life? Nobody wants that. Having a professional team to come alongside you and your WHY, keep you focused and on track will prove invaluable.

WILL

You need your WILL. This one is the simplest one to explain. If you don't have the will to do something… you won't do it.

Can you guess which one of these is most important? If you guessed your WILL, you're right! As I shared earlier, most people have their WHY. And you can put together an exceptional real estate team for yourself. But your WILL is solely dependent on you. If you don't make a move, it won't happen. If you don't respond, nothing will occur. If you don't do it, it won't get done. If your WILL is broken, it won't work. A broken WILL looks like this:

- Not completing your application with your loan officer
- Not returning phone calls or text messages to your Realtor
- Spending your down payment money on something less important- setting you back another several months
- Missing deadlines with the title or escrow company
- Not being able to make a decision or changing your mind over and over

These are just a few examples. And if you've done this in the past just say "ouch". But you might want to ask yourself, "Is my WILL broken?" Remember, you WHY and WISDOM are dependent on it.

So, let's do this. Let's fix your WILL right now.

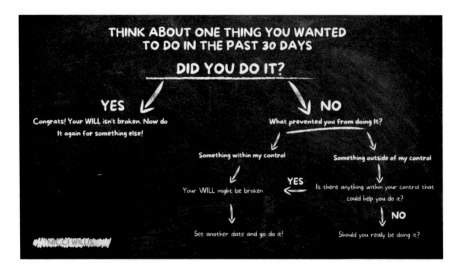

THINK ABOUT ONE THING YOU WANTED
TO DO IN THE PAST 30 DAYS

DID YOU DO IT?

YES — Congrats! Your WILL isn't broken. Now do it again for something else!

NO — What prevented you from doing it?

Something within my control

Something outside of my control

Your WILL might be broken

YES ← Is there anything within your control that could help you do it?

Set another date and go do it!

NO — Should you really be doing it?

As I shared with you earlier, your mindset has to be aligned first. Hopefully, you found these exercises helpful! P.S. They don't just work for buying a house. Feel free to use it when you're faced with anything you want to accomplish! And don't forget to refer back to these pages if you find yourself stuck at any time during this process. You CAN do it. It will take work. Having the right mindset will ensure you can accomplish your goal. Okay, let's prepare to buy your home.

PREPARATION

PREPARATION

Now, friend, I told you that most of this book would be about your mindset, changing the way you view the home buying process, and putting power back in your hands. But I think you'd be a tad bit disappointed with me if I didn't actually help you apply it. So, the next part of this book is going to be about walking you through the home buying process but most importantly, showing you some of the common hangups in each part of the process, what you should know about them, and how to overcome them.

It's important to keep in mind that no transaction is the same. Each one is different because we're all different and we are buying different houses. But I will help you to apply what works for you. Keep this book as a guide and reference during your home buying journey. If you stumble upon something, come back to this part of the book to see how you can handle it.

BEFORE WE GET STARTED

What not to do first

The first thing first-time homebuyers tend to do when they make the decision to buy a house is jump on Zillow or Realtor.com and start scrolling. I want to encourage you… do the absolute opposite! You're probably saying right now, "Too late, Nicci! I've already got an account!" That's okay. However, don't start any searches. Here's why. Have you ever had something happen to your body, and instead of calling the doctor first, you jumped on WebMD and began to self-diagnose yourself? Two hours later, you're ready to call your real doctor and tell them that you are 99% sure you either have a common cold or you need to have your left leg amputated. Well, that's what it's like when you bring your Zillow searches to a realtor. It's a self-diagnosis without the proper due diligence from a professional. A search on your own will likely give you misinformation, a limited or too large of a search pool, and most importantly (if you're not pre-approved for anything) time wasted. I want you to avoid this heartache and frustration altogether. Instead, I want you to focus on building your Home Buying Team.

How early should I start building my team?

It's never too early. Here's my rule of thumb. Start as early as 1 year from the time you plan to buy your house. That way, you can get ahead of anything that needs work: your credit score, down payment savings, and general knowledge about the process. But with your team in place, you have the right people to hold you accountable, give you advice, and celebrate your wins as you prepare for homeownership. Doing this alone is doable but not as effective if you really want to meet your goal.

Finding a Realtor

It's actually quite easy to find a good realtor. But it takes some work to find a great one. I want you to find a great one. And friend, some realtors aren't going to like what I say here but I'm going to say it anyway. You don't owe anyone your business just because they are related to you, are your friend, or were sent to you as a recommendation. As you build your Home Buying team, consider that you are hiring someone to work on your behalf. You want to make sure this person is a good fit for you. That they are not only knowledgeable about the market, but they can apply the market to your specific situation. That they are solution-bearers and can make it happen. How do you find a great realtor? Interviews. It is okay to interview a few realtors before you choose one. In fact, this will help you avoid a pitfall- working with more than one realtor. Friend, it is not okay to work with more than one realtor. When you enter into an agreement (whether written or verbal) with a realtor to find you a home, trust me, whether you know it or not, that realtor is going to get to work. However, if you contact another realtor "just in case" or to "keep your options open", my question to you is, are you serious about this process? You only need one home, and you only need one realtor to help you find it. Check out my "Questions to Ask When Hiring a Realtor" guide in the resources section on my website (BeforeYouBuyReadThis.com). Use it as a guide to help you interview realtors. Let them know you are interviewing other realtors (**Hint**: a great realtor will understand because they are interviewing you too). Once you've found/hired your realtor, let that realtor know you want to work with them AND let the others know you went with someone else. This will stop the additional follow-up calls.

> **POWER MOVE**: This is your first point of commitment in a line of things you will commit to in this process. Remember, you're buying a home, with a mortgage that you will live in for the foreseeable future. Take a deep breath and be okay with commitment.

Find a Loan Officer

Once you've added your realtor to your team, they are the ones who usually make recommendations on loan officers to contact based on your needs. Remember, you are building YOUR team. So do the same thing here. Interview! You know I've got you. There's a "Questions to Ask When Hiring a Loan Officer" Guide in the Resources section on my website (BeforeYouBuyReadThis.com). Use it as a guide to help you interview loan officers. Let them know you are interviewing other loan officers. They should understand.

What to expect

During this part of the home buying process, you are working primarily with your loan officer. They will ask you for a lot of documentation. This is good. But I'm going to be honest. This is part of the process. If you find yourself overwhelmed or experiencing any of these hangups, here's some encouragement. Read them aloud:

1. I am confident in my ability to find the ideal home for myself and my family.

2. I attract positive opportunities and resources that support my home buying journey.

3. My ideal home is within reach, and I am taking steps to make it a reality.

4. I am financially prepared and responsible, ensuring a smooth home buying process.

5. I trust my instincts and make wise decisions throughout my home search.

6. I am deserving of a beautiful and comfortable home that meets all my needs.

7. The right home is waiting for me, and I am guided to it effortlessly.

8. I release any fear or doubt and embrace excitement and optimism in my home buying journey.

9. I am open to receiving guidance and support from professionals and loved ones.

10. My new home is a place of safety, joy, and growth for me and my family.

Don't give up. Keep communicating with your loan officer. They've been there before and can work with you and give you advice on how to find what you need to give to them.

Getting Funded

There are two ways to pay for a home. You can pay cash, or you can get financed. The majority of first-time home buyers are getting financed. Financing means you are getting a mortgage loan. In order to get pre-approved for a mortgage you need to meet with a loan officer. Here are the 3 most common mortgage loans available and what you need to be approved:

Types of Mortgage Loans

	FHA	Conventional	VA
Insurer	Backed by Government	Not backed by Government	Backed by the Government
Down Payment	As low as 3.5%	As low as 5%-20%	No Down Payment
Credit Score	More Lenient As low as 580*	More Strict As low as 620	More Lenient
Debt-to-Income Ratio	up to 50%	More Strict up to 43%	Very Strict up to 41%
Mortgage Insurance (aka MIP or PMI)	Requires upfront mortgage insurance AND mortgage insurance for the life of the loan	Not required if you put 20% down. Will cancel once you reach 20% equity	No PMI
Loan Limits	Borrow up to $498,257 for a single-family home	Borrow up to $766,500 for a single-family home	No limit
Interest Rates	Slightly higher	Slightly lower (especially if you have an excellent credit score)	Current market rates
Property Requirements	Properties must meet certain minimum standards set by the FHA- safety, soundness, and livability requirements.	Less strict	Must be primary residence Cant skip inspections

Delayed but Not Denied

So now that you know the minimum amounts you need to get funded, what happens when you don't have one or more of these items and it's a "No"? You finally decided to buy a house, you started building your Home Buying Team, you've met with a Realtor and a loan officer, and you've turned in all of these documents, all for your loan officer to say, "Well, we can't pre-approve you right now". Look, it happens. And if this is you, let me give you some encouragement. A "no" is not forever. If you don't get pre-approved for your home right away this doesn't change the fact that you decided to buy a home. You still want to buy a home. A "no" on a pre-approval is what I like to affectionately call a "not yet". Yes, it stings. But in reality, it's the start to your game plan; showing you the holes that you need to work on in order to become pre-approved. Friend, can I tell you something? This is a stumbling block that I see all the time. I can't tell you how many times I've seen people choose to give up at this point in the journey.

Let me tell you right here and right now: There is nothing that can't be fixed. Even the worst credit scores can be fixed within 12 to 18 months. I've seen it and I've also been there. Yes, I, Nicci Willis, ruined my credit score TWICE and rebuilt it. I'm being transparent to let you know that you can do it too. Don't have the savings for your down payment that you desire to have?

There's nothing that a little discipline and some creative thinking won't do to get you the money you need for the down payment on your house. Do you have a birthday coming up? Instead of gifts, ask for people to give to your "New Home Down Payment Fund" and promise them a big shindig and an invite to your housewarming party. Make it a challenge between you and your spouse or your partner to see how much extra money you can make to add to your home down payment fund. And I'll give you a hint: a great loan officer will tell you they can't pre-approve you BUT they will also tell you what you need in order to get there. That's the perfect way to create your game plan. Then, keep following up with your loan officer. Ask them to check in on you to see how you are doing. As your realtor, I will get the notification as well. I love accountability. A great realtor will come alongside you and give you that extra layer of accountability, checking in from time to time to make sure you reach that goal. These are just a couple of examples of how you can take a temporary "No" and turn it into a "Go" in a short time. The key here is don't stop moving. Use that "no" as motivation to get you where you need to be. Finally, hang in there and keep reading this book… because I believe you'll still need it, future home buyer.

Pre-qualification vs. Pre-approval

These two sound similar but they are not the same. A pre-qualification is a preliminary check completed by your loan officer just to see if you could qualify to purchase a home. Oftentimes there is no hard credit pull (an inquiry will not show up on your credit report) and they don't usually collect a lot of documentation. A pre-approval letter requires a more in-depth qualification process. It's going to require more documentation, you will get a hard credit pull (there will be an inquiry on your credit report), and the loan officer is also going to see how much house you can afford and or how much you want to pay per month for your home. They will check your debt-to-income ratio (how much debt you have versus how much income and assets you have), your employment history, bank statements, etc. This is because a pre-approval letter means that they have vetted you and they are willing to give you a home loan to purchase your home. As your realtor, in order to show you homes, I need a pre-approval letter. A pre-qualification letter is not going to get us in the door. Let's put it this way, a pre-qualification letter says, "Based on what we see, we *think* we can give this person a mortgage for this amount". A pre-approval letter says, "Based on what we see, we *know* we can give this person a mortgage for this amount, and we are ready to back it up". Make this easy for yourself and ask your loan officer for a pre-approval letter.

THE HOME
BUYING
PROCESS

THE HOME BUYING PROCESS

So, you've gotten your pre-approval letter. What happens next?

Time to Go Shopping!

First, we look at your criteria based on what you can afford and make sure it's realistic. Here are some questions to ask yourself.

1. Does my search criteria (location, number of bedrooms, home features, etc.) line up with my budget?

2. If not, what are my "need-to-haves" vs. my "nice-to-haves"?

3. If my "need-to-haves" are not within my budget, do I need to increase my budget or become more realistic for the budget I have?

I Don't Believe in "Dream Homes" and Neither Should You

I know you've heard it before because I hear it all the time. A Realtor promising to get you into your "dream home". Or an ad on TV telling you to get pre-approved with their lender so you can buy your "dream home". Or maybe you've said it before. "I want to buy my dream home." I'm going to keep it real. That narrative is setting you up for disappointment and paints a picture that everything has to be perfect. You might find the perfect house but is it in your budget? What if five other buyers believe it's their *perfect house* too? And it turns into a bidding war? And I guarantee you when you find the perfect house there will always be one better. You might be thinking, "Geez Nicci, why are you raining on my Parade?" Trust me I'm not raining on your parade. I'm only bringing a little reality so we can look at buying a home from a healthy, realistic perspective. It's rare that the first home you see, you fall in love with, write up an offer that's immediately accepted with no counter offers, and you close on it in less than 30 days. There are a lot of moving parts. This is only the beginning. Spare yourself on the emotional roller coaster. Instead of thinking about buying your dream home, focus on buying your *ideal* home. Think about how long you plan to stay there. What you plan to do with the home if you ever decide to move. Do you plan to get married? Do you plan to start a family? Do you plan to have pets? Do you plan to do a lot of traveling? Do you plan to host guests often? Don't worry I've made this super easy guide on things to think about for your ideal home for you in the resources section of my website (BeforeYouBuyReadThis.com). What I'm saying might feel harsh, but I'm not in the business of showing homes just to show them. My job is to help you reach your goal of becoming a homeowner.

Now back to the home search…

Based on your criteria, I'm going to create a search portal that reflects exactly what we've talked about within the price range and location. I know search portals get a bad reputation because it feels like we're just putting you on a search and we are just setting it and forgetting it. But believe me, your search portal is helpful. Yes, there are other ways you can search for a home. Like through Realtor.com or Zillow but here's what these third-party sites don't tell you. They get their information from the multiple listing service. Most of the time it takes a while for that information from the multiple listing service to port over to these third-party sites and oftentimes, what you are seeing is outdated and incorrect information. You can also drive around and find homes for sale. Here's why that can be a problem: Realtors are able to search based on your pre-approval letter. Some homes don't accept FHA Loans. There are some homes that can be in Probate and that can take up to 12 months to resolve. So still the best and most accurate way is to go through the realtor's search portal, look at what you're getting there, and adjust. One of your most underutilized tools is to ask questions. You can ask me why a particular home didn't appear in your search portal. I can tell you why based on your criteria. Sometimes it's a quick change to include a specific type of home. Other times, I might tell you why that home and homes like it wouldn't fit your criteria and why it can't change. Here's what I don't want. I don't want you to assume that we realtors just put you on a random search and forgot about you. The search also helps me as a realtor see what's working and what's not working. If you're searching on third-party sites I can't see what you like and what you don't like. Open communication is the only way this relationship can be successful.

Still not finding the homes you like?

If you're still not finding homes that you like or you're finding them a bit lackluster here are two options.

1. Go back to your "need-to-haves" and "nice-to-haves" lists. You may need to make some adjustments.

2. Go back to your loan officer and see if you can increase what you're pre-approved for. Just remember if you increase your pre-approval, you're also increasing your down payment, your monthly mortgage payments, and other costs.

Time to tour

Once you start finding homes you like in the search, it's time to build your tour. Realtors like to help clients build tours in different ways, but I will tell you mine. For the first time, we are going to look at your top 3-5 homes. This may or may not include some you've chosen and some I have chosen based on some insight I may have. You might be thinking, "Nicci, I've got time. Why not 10 or 12?" Remember, we are searching for your ideal home. If you want to see 10 homes during your first tour, my question to you is, have you narrowed down enough? And how serious are you about purchasing right now? You only need one home. Don't shoot the messenger! This is not to say that over time we won't look at more than that amount to find your ideal home. But the first tour is usually spent fine-tuning what you think you desire in a home. You might realize you actually prefer a traditional floor plan to an open one. You might find out that a fixer-upper really isn't what you want.

You might decide that a 2-car garage will work just as well as a 3-car garage. Just know, I'm taking notes the whole time. And each tour after that should bring you closer and closer if not to an exact match of your top "need-to-haves" list, of course.

> **Power move:** Remember this when home shopping. Paint is a choice. So are furniture and decor. Don't let the homeowner's personal style deter you from what could potentially be your home. Ask yourself, *"Does this check off the 'need-to-haves' list?"* So maybe a red accent wall wouldn't be your choice, but the rest of the home is ideal. A bucket of paint and a weekend project could make that red wall go away. That's also why I'm there. To help give you perspective.

We Found Your Ideal Home! Now What?

Once we find a home you like, our next step is to write an offer. An offer is simply a written contract you present to the seller. If the seller agrees to the terms, they sign it and you are officially "under contract" to purchase the home. More often than not, you might need to negotiate a little. If the seller doesn't agree with your terms they can send you a counteroffer. Depending on the season or the type of market, you could have some competition with other buyers and be in multiple offers. I'm saying this to say: watch out for this next pitfall. Don't get too emotionally attached. Until your name is on the deed, it is just a house. Then and only then, can you make it your home.

You Win Some and You Lose Some

No one is going to tell you how heartbreaking it feels to lose a deal on the house you thought would be "the one". It's a gut punch. I've been in real estate for over 13 years and it's still tough. Here's how I've learned to shake it off faster.

1. Acknowledge it sucks

2. Know that there's another one coming and stay true to your "need-to-haves" list

3. Get back out there and keep going

You may feel the need to panic if you've been searching for a while. To avoid this, talk to your realtor. Ask if there should be something else you could be doing. The market may have changed since you first began. If your search is very specific, it might need time. Just know it might take a few offers to win one. Stay open and stay in communication with your realtor.

Once you win a contract, it feels great! You should take a minute to celebrate… okay that's enough. Maybe I made you laugh. It's funny but I'm serious. Because now it's time to get into the details.

DOWN PAYMENT VS. EARNEST MONEY DEPOSIT VS. CLOSING COSTS

These three always get confused. And yes, as a Realtor, it's our fault. We just don't do a good job explaining it. But I'm going to settle this once and for all. You ready? Here we go:

Down Payment

Unless you are getting VA financing or paying cash, you will most likely have a down payment. Your down payment is based on your pre-approval letter. It can range between 3%-20% but it can be lower if you get down payment assistance. We will discuss that later. To simplify my example, we will go with 3.5%. So if you purchase a home for $300,000 your down payment is $10,500. You must have this money in your bank account ready to bring to the table (with today's technology, you will wire the funds from your bank to the escrow company) when you close on your home. This isn't the only money you must have. Stay with me.

Earnest Money Deposit

Your earnest money deposit is an amount that you give to the escrow company to hold on to when (and only when) your contract is accepted that says, "Hey I'm serious about purchasing this property". There are two important things to remember about this:

1. It can be whatever amount you want it to be. But remember, you're telling the seller you're serious about your offer. Typically, I see 1% of the purchase price. So, we will go with that for our example (1% of $300,000= $3000).

2. This earnest money deposit *comes out of your down payment* and *goes toward the purchase price* of the home at closing. So, you put $3000 down now to say you're serious, then you need to bring the remainder of the down payment ($7,500) to the closing table.

You might be asking, *"Nicci, what if something happens? Can I get my earnest money deposit back?"* Short answer, yes. There are specific time frames where you could get your money back. Here are three:

- During your due diligence period (usually the first 7-10 days of the contract but this is negotiable)

- If there is an HOA, during the Common-Interest Community Contingency (5 calendar days from receiving the resale package in Nevada)

- If the seller cancels the contract outside of a contingency period

There may be other times based on the state in which you live. You will want to consult with your Realtor for your case.

Closing Costs

Mortgage closing costs are fees and expenses you pay when you secure a loan for your home, beyond the down payment. These costs are generally 3% to 5% of the loan amount and may include title insurance, Escrow company fees, appraisals, taxes, HOA fees, and more.

You WILL have closing costs in addition to your down payment. The key is to make sure you have saved for it. I've got a simple Savings Calculator in the Resources Page on my website beforeyoubuyreadthis.com to estimate how much you should save for your home.

Due Diligence Period

The Due Diligence period is the time period you have to get the property inspected and decide if you want to move forward with the purchase, or ask for repairs. Check out my video on the due diligence period. I'll keep it simple. NEVER skip this step. Inspections usually range from $400-$700 depending on the depth of the inspection. This is a cost you pay up front. Now, here you might be saying "Wow, Nicci, another expense?" Put it this way, it's worth every penny when you think about spending $500 to avoid a half-million-dollar problem. You'll want to hire a third-party professional inspection company. Don't worry about finding one. We Realtors are quite resourceful! However, as your Realtor, I can only give you a list of companies to research. I can't choose your inspection company for you. That is a conflict of interest, so don't ask me.

Your inspector is looking at everything in the property from the roof to the foundation and everything in between. *Warning* They WILL find something. It's their job and no property is perfect. You just have to determine your "deal breakers" with your Realtor, and your Realtor will have some suggestions as well. Remember, you're not alone in this.

What's Everyone Else Doing?

Good question! Here's what your real estate team is doing in the background: Your loan officer is getting more documentation from you, putting your entire financial story together, and preparing to send the entire transaction to the Underwriter for approval. Think of this person as the Wizard from The Wizard of Oz. You will never see or speak to this person, but they control a large part of this transaction. Their ultimate approval is the key to getting your home. We want to give them what they need to approve your full financial story and underwrite the loan for your mortgage. Your loan officer is also reminding you NOT to quit your job, open a credit card, buy a car, or do ANYTHING with your credit. Why, because it can ruin your entire deal! When they ask for documentation, don't wait. Send it in. You don't want to be the one to delay the purchase.

The escrow company is holding the earnest money deposit. They are also researching the property to make sure there are no liens against the property, there are no other claims to the property, and it has a clean title. They are also preparing to transition the title and deed into your name.

My team is making sure we stay on task working from a checklist and sending you reminders so that we close escrow on or before the contracted date. And I am checking in on you. During this time, we are about half way through the transaction. I'm answering questions you might have. I'm asking about your wellbeing (because it can get emotional sometimes). I'm checking with the other real estate team members to make sure we are still on time. I might be troubleshooting to keep the transaction as stress-free as possible.

The appraisal is when the bank or mortgage company (these names are sometimes used interchangeably- for simplicity, we will use the word Mortgage Company) confirms that the purchase price you've agreed to pay for the house is actually worth that amount. Why is this important? Because the mortgage company will only provide funds for the loan based upon how much the house is worth.

How do appraisals work?

The mortgage company hires a third-party real estate agent to compare homes that have sold with similar square footage, number of rooms, bathrooms, etc. There are three results that can happen after an appraisal. I'll give you an example to help you compare the three. Let's say the purchase price for your ideal home $400,000. Both you and the seller have agreed. GREAT! We're under contract. Now it's time for the appraisal:

1. The property appraises UNDER value- (example) The purchase price is $400,000 but it only appraises for $390,000; a $10,000 difference. The mortgage company will only provide the loan amount for $390,000. With this knowledge, you have a few options: pay the difference out of pocket, renegotiate the purchase price with the seller to match the lower appraisal value, or cancel the contract. None of these are great options for either side.

2. The property appraises AT value- (example) The purchase price is $400,000 and it appraises for $400,000. Congratulations! We move forward! No further action is needed.

3. The property appraises ABOVE value- (example) The purchase price is $400,000 and it appraises for $410,000! Whoohoo! This is the BEST case scenario! Not only do we move forward, but you will walk into your new home with equity!

How often do either of these options happen? It depends on the market. Just know, the goal is to purchase a home that appraises at value.

I'm Buying a Home in an HOA... Help!

Not to worry. Depending on where you live, HOAs (aka Common Interest Communities or CICs) might not be very popular. I'm originally from Cincinnati where gated communities and HOAs are not as popular. Now I live in Vegas, where about 75% of homes are within some sort of HOA and it's highly probable that if you move here, you'll be in one. If you don't want a home within an HOA we can avoid them during our home search.

During the transaction, there is a specific time when you will review the resale package. This is all the information about the HOA, how they operate, who is in charge, and most importantly what you can and can't do with your property. You will also receive a demand package. This document will tell you if the property you're purchasing is in right standing with the HOA. For instance, if the property has past violations or if they have any past-due amounts. In the State of Nevada, you get 5 calendar days to review these documents and determine whether you agree or disagree with being part of the HOA. Simply put: if you agree you move forward with the transaction. If you disagree, you cancel the contract. Just know all HOAs have rules and you'll probably want to determine before shopping if living in an HOA is right for you so you don't waste your time or your money. Be sure to check out my full video on Navigating HOAs on my website at Beforeyoubuyreadthis.com.

The Home Stretch

At this point you are almost to the finish line. What's next?

Order your insurance. Much like the inspection, I cannot pick the insurance company for you. I have a list to give you of reputable companies. But here's a great tip: if you're happy with your current car or rental insurance, call them first. Oftentimes, they are able to give you a discount when you bundle more than one product with them. Once you've done this, the insurance company will send a declaration page to the escrow company and part of your closing costs will include the first year's premium.

Order your Home Warranty. Again, much like the inspection and homeowners' insurance, I cannot pick the insurance company for you. But I can give you a list of reputable companies. Home warranties cover large appliances like stoves, refrigerators, HVAC systems, pool pumps, etc. Depending on the type of package you choose, home warranties usually cost up to $600 for the first year. This is not an upfront cost but is invoiced into your closing costs. Check out my full video on home warranties vs. home-owners' insurance on the Resources Page on my website at Beforeyoubuyreadthis.com.

The next thing is getting a Clear to Close from the Underwriter at the mortgage company. Essentially, the underwriter has processed your entire financial story and is confident that you will pay your loan back. Everyone receives this email and breathes a big sigh of relief. It's GO TIME! Once this happens, your loan officer will do two things:

1. Send you your closing documents to review.

2. Send all of their documents to the escrow company who then balances the debits and credits on both the buyer and seller sides of the transaction and calculates who needs to wire funds at closing and who will receive funds at closing. Typically, as the buyer, you will need to wire funds.

Final Days Until Closing

In the final 2-3 days prior to the closing, we will review your estimated settlement statement. You'll be able to see all the costs you agreed to pay, any costs the seller agreed to pay, your homeowners insurance costs, home warranty cost, escrow fees, loan origination fees, county recording fees, and a host of other fees. The most important number is at the bottom that shows, after all the debits and credits, how much money you need to wire to the escrow company to close on your house. A good realtor will make sure you have your settlement statement. A great realtor will review it with you.

We will schedule your final walkthrough. Don't skip your final walkthrough. Why? This is the only time you get to recheck and make sure the property is in the same condition it was in when you entered the transaction (WOW! Almost about a whole month ago!). You also want to make sure (if you requested repairs) that the repairs were properly done. Once you've closed on the home it is now in your possession. It's yours. No takebacks! And you can't require the seller (or previous owner) to fix anything then. Visit my website for a free download of the final walkthrough checklist on my Resource Page at Beforeyoubuyreadthis.com.

Closing Day

Before we talk about the closing, let's do an exercise first. After being part of so many transactions, I've seen different reactions from my clients (some good and some bad) and oftentimes it had nothing to do with how good or bad the transaction went but everything to do with their expectations. One thing is certain, there is no perfect transaction.

I want you to imagine what you expect this day to look like for you and take control of the day before it is here.

I am prepared for the day.
I can only control how I react to situations. And I react with positivity.
There is a solution to everything.
Everything is working out for my good.
My team is for me.
I am not alone.

Now that our mindset is set, here is what you will need on signing day:

The good thing about technology is that most documentation that was required for you to bring, you've already submitted electronically or via email prior to closing. So, this is pretty simple. Bring the following:

1. Your I.D.

2. ME! Yes, me. A good realtor will make sure you are there for your signing. A great realtor will make sure you are there with representation. Sometimes, for whatever reason, we can't physically be there. But even if your realtor can't be there, he or she should make sure you have representation there for your signing. Someone who can ask questions on your behalf, make sure you understand everything you are signing, and keep you calm during the process.

Here's a tip: Dress nicely- usually your team will want to take pictures. It's a big day! So, get dressed and show up for your big day!

What do you leave with?

A copy of the paperwork you just signed.

Your wire instructions to wire the remaining balance you saw at the bottom of yur settlement statement if you haven't done so before signing.

Conclusion

Well Friend, how do you feel? As we wrap up this journey together, I can't help but feel a sense of gratitude for having shared this experience with you. From the very beginning, we dove into the depths of the home buying process, exploring everything from mindset to the nitty-gritty details of finding the right realtor and securing funding.

We started with the foundation of mindset—understanding our why, harnessing wisdom, and fortifying our will. Because let's face it, embarking on this journey requires more than just financial readiness; it demands a resilient spirit and a clear vision of what we're striving for.

Then, we delved into preparation, ensuring that we armed ourselves with the right tools and knowledge to navigate the complexities of the market. Finding the right Realtor and loan officer became pivotal steps, as they were our guides through the maze of options and decisions.

And what a journey it was! From the exhilarating highs of getting pre-approved to the nail-biting moments of waiting for the final days to closing, we've experienced it all. But through it all, we've grown, we've learned, and we've become more empowered homeowners-to-be.

Here's to new beginnings, to dreams realized, and to the joy of holding those keys in our hands. Congratulations, my friend. Our journey may be coming to an end, but your adventure as a homeowner is just beginning.

One Final Thing

As we close the chapter on this incredible journey together, I want to express my deepest gratitude for allowing me to guide you along your journey. Your support, your enthusiasm, and your trust have meant the world to me.

Now, as we stand on the brink of new adventures, I have one final request. I need YOUR help. Whether you're ready to take the plunge into the home buying process yourself or if you know someone who is, I would be honored to be your realtor, guiding you through every step of the way. Not in the Las Vegas area? No problem! Allow me to help you find the perfect realtor in your area. It's the least I can do for all your support.

In the world of real estate, referrals are the lifeblood of our business. So, if you've found value in our journey together, if you believe in the service and expertise I've provided, I humbly ask for your support in spreading the word.

Together, let's continue to make your goals a reality, one home at a time.

With heartfelt appreciation,

Nicci

P.S. Don't forget, our team is here to help! No matter the location or stage you're in. Schedule your 30-minute free chat with The Willis Team at thewillisteamlv. com and let's help you become a homeowner!

Find all resources discussed in the book and many more on the website Beforeyoubuyreadthis.com